T0129176

THE PRACTICAL STRATEGIES SERIES
IN GIFTED EDUCATION

series editors
FRANCES A. KARNES & KRISTEN R. STEPHENS

Motivating
Gifted Students

Del Siegle & D. Betsy McCoach

Routledge
Taylor & Francis Group
NEW YORK AND LONDON

First published 2005 by Prufrock Press Inc.

Published 2021 by Routledge
605 Third Avenue, New York, NY 10017
2 Park Square, Milton Park, Abingdon, Oxon OX14 4RN

Routledge is an imprint of the Taylor & Francis Group, an informa business

ISBN 13: 978-1-59363-015-7 (pbk)

Contents

Series Preface

The *Practical Strategies Series in Gifted Education* offers teachers, counselors, administrators, parents, and other interested parties with up-to-date instructional techniques and information on a variety of issues pertinent to the field of gifted education. Each guide addresses a focused topic and is written by scholars with authority on the issue. Several guides have been published. Among the titles are:

- *Acceleration Strategies for Teaching Gifted Learners*
- *Curriculum Compacting: An Easy Start to Differentiating for High-Potential Students*
- *Enrichment Opportunities for Gifted Learners*
- *Independent Study for Gifted Learners*
- *Motivating Gifted Students*
- *Questioning Strategies for Teaching the Gifted*
- *Social & Emotional Teaching Strategies*
- *Using Media & Technology With Gifted Learners*

For a current listing of available guides within the series, please contact Prufrock Press at (800) 998-2208 or visit http://www.prufrock.com.

Author Preface

Much of our thinking about motivation has been shaped by our work at the National Research Center on the Gifted and Talented. We wish to acknowledge the contributions of other members of our research team: Sally M. Reis, Meredith Greene, Fredric Schreiber, and Rebecca Mann. This research is supported under the Educational Research and Development Centers Program, PR/Award Number R206R000001, as administered by the Institute of Education Sciences, U.S. Department of Education. The findings and opinions expressed in this publication do not reflect the position or policies of the Institute of Education Sciences or the U.S. Department of Education. Some of the content in this publication appears in an article prepared for *Teaching Exceptional Children*.

Introduction

All individuals have the ability to learn and attain self-fulfill-
ment; however, many children are at risk of failing to achieve
their academic potential. Although gifted students are one
group of exceptional learners who are not normally considered
at risk for academic failure, the seeming lack of motivation of
many academically gifted students is an area of concern and
frustration for many teachers, parents, and counselors. Why do
some students who seem capable of outstanding performance
fail to realize their potential? What causes some gifted students
to be more motivated than others? Are there strategies educators and parents can implement to motivate students to achieve
academically?

Extensive research in educational psychology has demonstrated the relationship between four factors (task value, self-
efficacy, environmental perceptions, and self-regulation) and
achievement. This publication describes these four factors and
provides specific strategies that educators and parents can use to
help motivate gifted students toward academic achievement.

While there are many factors that contribute to achievement, motivated students appear to exhibit three key perceptions and a resultant behavior (see Figure 1). First and foremost, students find value in their school experience. School is meaningful for them. Motivated students enjoy what they are doing or believe that what they are doing will produce beneficial outcomes. Second, they believe they have the skills to be successful. Third, they trust their environment and expect they can succeed in it. When students value the task or outcome and have positive perceptions of themselves and their opportunities for success, they are more likely to implement self-regulatory behavior by setting realistic expectations and applying appropriate strategies for academic success.

Some of these four components may play a stronger influence than others. Strength in one area can sometimes compensate for a weakness in another, but, overall, motivated individuals possess all four components. Although these four components are internal to the student, contextual and situational factors exert a great deal of influence on students' development of each of the four components. Teachers and the curriculum they present, the attitudes and activities of peers, and the attitudes and activities within their homes influence students' perceptions of the four components presented in Figure 1.

This publication focuses on student attitudes and suggests strategies educators and parents can use that promote student motivation. However, low academic achievement can sometimes be indicative of a more serious physical, mental, or emotional issue. Moon and Hall (1998) noted that endogenous factors such as learning disabilities, attention-deficit/hyperactivity disorder, hearing impairment, nontraditional learning styles, and emotional problems can contribute to underachievement. Therefore, gifted students who are having difficulty with school should be screened for a wide variety of physical, mental, or emotional problems before focusing on motivation issues (Siegle & McCoach, 2002).

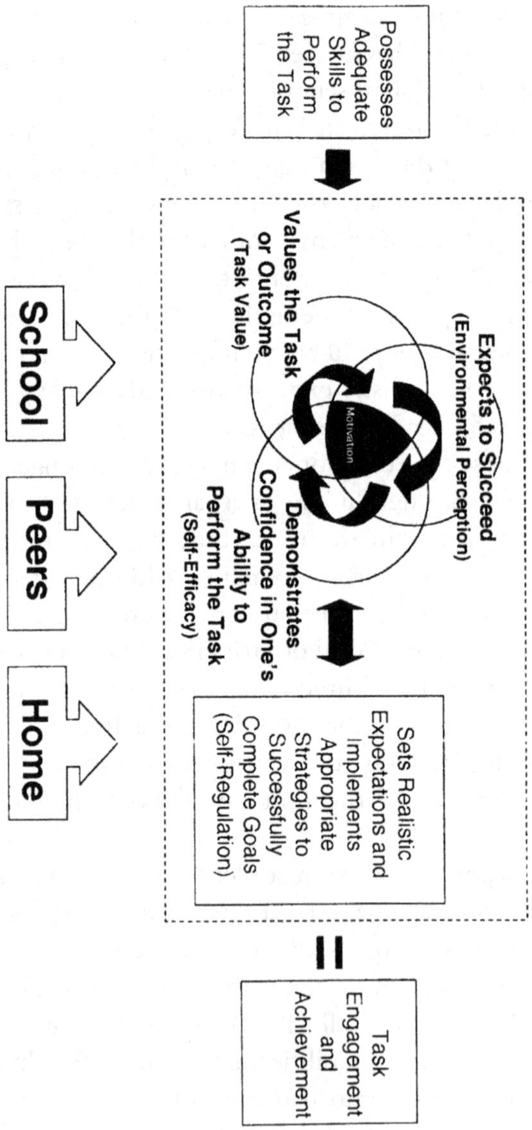

Figure 1. Siegle and McCoach Achievement Orientation Model

First and foremost, students must value academics. They must view school as useful, purposeful, and interesting. Sometimes, gifted students appear to be unmotivated to complete their schoolwork or to engage in classroom activities. Begin by reframing this problem as a general question. What motivates a person to put forth effort to accomplish a given task?

There are two basic reasons that a person engages in an activity. Either the person enjoys the activity or the person values the outcome or byproduct of the activity in some way. For example, video games, romance novels, and movies may be enjoyable activities. While the act of doing laundry or washing dishes may not be enjoyable, having clean clothes to wear or clean dishes in the cabinet pleases most people more than wearing dirty clothes or having moldy dishes in the sink. Therefore, in this example, even though one may not enjoy the act of cleaning as much as watching TV, one engages in this activity because it is seen as a necessary step in the quest for a clean house. When individuals value either the task itself or the outcome of the task, they obtain the prerequisite motivation necessary to engage in that task. If a person finds no value in the act of completing the task and does not value its outcome, that task has no value for the individual and it is unlikely that he or she will engage in it. For example, there would be very little value in sorting the garbage by color. The activity of sorting garbage is not enjoyable to most people, and having color-coded garbage doesn't seem to be particularly beneficial. Therefore, sorting garbage by color has very little task value.

Achievement values are "the incentives or purposes that individuals have for succeeding on a given task" (Wigfield, 1994, p. 102). According to the expectancy-value theory, motivation is the product of expectancy for success and the value of the incentive (Boggiano & Pittman, 1992). In other words, the value a person places on either the task or the outcome and the perceived probability of success determines the amount of effort the person will exert in attempting to complete the task successfully. The motivation for engaging in the task is largely determined by the subjective value the person places on the task or the accomplishment (Bandura, 1986). For example, two people may hold the same belief that their behavior will result in a particular outcome, but they may evaluate the attractiveness of that outcome quite differently (Bandura). The person who places greater value on the outcome or finds the outcome more attractive will be more motivated to achieve.

Value may even compensate for low probability of success. People often put forth effort when they place high value on an outcome even when they believe that the likelihood of success is quite low. For example, due to the extremely high value attached to the outcome, individuals are motivated to enter sweepstakes or buy lottery tickets even though there is an extremely low probability of success. As the jackpot becomes larger, more people buy lottery tickets even though the probability of winning the lottery remains extremely low. This example demonstrates the power of value in determining behavior. Students' achievement values affect their self-regulation and motivation (Wigfield, 1994) because their goals influence how they approach, engage in, and respond to academic tasks (Hidi & Harackiewicz, 2000). "When students value a task, they will be more likely to engage in it, expend more effort on it, and do better on it" (Wigfield, p. 102).

Some students are not motivated to achieve in school because they do not value the outcomes of school, nor do they enjoy completing schoolwork. To reverse underachievement that stems from an apparent lack of motivation, educators must first determine how to build task value into the student's scholastic experiences.

Eccles and Wigfield (1995), two leading researchers in the field of motivation, expanded Atkinson's expectancy value model to include a variety of achievement-related influences that impact individuals' expectancies and values (Wigfield, 1994). In particular, they hypothesized that students' motivation to complete tasks stems from three task values: the attainment (identity), utility (usefulness now and in the future), and intrinsic (interest and relevance) values associated with the task.

In other words, three students may value a given task for different reasons. Consider a U.S. history class that is covering the Revolutionary War. One student may value the class because he views himself as a scholar who does well in school, whatever the class. Engaging in the task is important to his conception of who he is. Another may be seeking high grades in order to obtain a college scholarship. A third student may value the class because she is interested in the Revolutionary War. While each of these students is motivated to do well in the history class, each is valuing it for a different reason. The next section will explore each of these types of valuation in more depth. Examples of how educators and parents can increase student motivation by addressing each type of task value are provided.

Attainment (Identity) Value

Attainment value is the importance students attach to the task as it relates to their conception of their identity and ideals (Eccles & Wigfield, 1995). Attainment value relates the importance individuals attach to a given task to broader, core values they have about themselves (Wigfield, 1994). These central values contribute to whether students view specific activities as meaningful.

For example, students who identify themselves as athletes set goals related to their sport. Students who pride themselves on being good students seek good grades and test scores as affirmation. These students are motivated to attain the goals because they are associated with their perceptions of who they are. Impacting a student's attainment value is likely to be more difficult than impacting a student's intrinsic or utility values because identity value is linked with a person's core perceptions and values about him- or herself, which are usually almost fully formed by adolescence. However, students tend to internalize the values of their family, friends, and other influential adults with whom they identify. Therefore, providing students with models who value academic achievement may increase attainment value. Rimm (1995) suggested that effective models often share something in common with the student and often are of the same gender. According to Rimm (2001), identification with a role model is based on three variables: "(1) *nurturance*, or the warmth of the relationship between the child and a particular adult; (2) *similarities* that children see between themselves and an adult; and (3) the *power* of the adult as perceived by the child" (p. 27).

Motivation Tips

- Educators and parents can personalize the school experience by helping students integrate academic goals into their ideals. Students bring a variety of experiences to the classroom, and learning becomes personally meaningful when students' prior knowledge and diverse experiences are connected with their present learning experiences.

• Educators and parents can provide students with role models who value academics.

Utility (Usefulness) Value

Utility value is how the task relates to present or future goals. While students may not enjoy an activity, they may value a later reward or outcome it produces (Wigfield, 1994). The activity must be integral to their vision of the future or instrumental to their pursuit of other goals. Because goals can play a key role in attaining later outcomes, educators and parents should help students see beyond the immediate activity to the long-term benefits it produces. Teachers need to be able to answer the common query, "Why do we have to study this stuff?"

Research on gifted underachievers has demonstrated the importance of valuing academic and career goals on students' eventual reversal of their underachievement. Peterson (2000) followed achieving and underachieving gifted high school students into college. She found that achievers' early certainty about career direction suggests that having aspirations and future goals may encourage academic achievement. Emerick (1992) reported that former underachievers were able to reverse their underachievement through the development of attainable goals that were both personally motivating and directly related to academic success.

One way to increase the value of the task is to reinforce students positively for completing the task. Extrinsic motivation is the motive to complete an activity to receive a reward or positive reinforcement that is external to the activity itself. Extrinsic motivators include rewards such as stickers, praise, grades, special privileges, prizes, money, material rewards, adult attention, or peer admiration. Teachers should use extrinsic motivators carefully, as Lepper's overjustification hypothesis suggests that providing extrinsic rewards for an intrinsically motivating activity can decrease a person's subsequent intrinsic motivation for that activity (Pintrich & Schunk, 1996).

Motivation Tips

- Parents and educators can help students see beyond the present activity to the long-term benefits it produces. A school assignment may seem unimportant, but acceptance into a prestigious university, earning a lucrative college scholarship, or obtaining a rewarding occupation may be outcomes that students value and are willing to strive toward.

- Teachers can help students see the usefulness of what they are learning by explicitly stating the purpose for and importance of lessons and assignments. At the beginning of every unit, teachers should explain why mastering these skills or learning this information is important to students. Before every lesson, state "why we are learning about this and how it is useful" in one or two sentences.

- Teachers can invite community members into the classroom. Such individuals can tie the school curriculum to their career activities. Parents can share how they use various skills learned in school.

- Teachers should relate the activities in their classrooms to the objectives of the course (Brophy, 1998). Show how classroom activities match the instructional goals of the class. "If teachers help students understand the overall goals of the course and how those goals are consistent with their own goals and interests, students may better understand and appreciate the importance and usefulness of a particular activity" (Morrone & Schutz, 2000, p. 154).

Intrinsic (Interest) Value

Intrinsic value often results from the enjoyment an activity produces for the participant (Wigfield, 1994). When students enjoy scholastic tasks, they are intrinsically motivated to do well. Both interests and personal relevance produce intrinsic value. Generally, students are intrinsically motivated to pursue activities that are moderately novel, interesting, enjoyable, exciting, and optimally challenging. When schoolwork is too easy, students become bored; when it is too difficult, they become frustrated and anxious (Deci & Ryan, 1985).

Teachers should try to create classroom environments that foster intrinsic motivation by providing students with opportunities to engage in interesting, personally relevant, challenging activities. In one study, researchers used self-selected enrichment projects based on students' interests as a systematic intervention for underachieving gifted students. This approach specifically targeted student strengths and interests and helped reverse academic underachievement in more than half of the sample (Baum, Renzulli, & Hébert, 1995). Emerick (1992) also found underachievers responded well to "interventions incorporating educational modifications which focus on individual strengths and interests" (p. 140).

Motivation Tips

- Teachers can learn about student interests and integrate these interests into classroom instruction and curricula.

- Whenever possible, teachers should offer students authentic choices about the ways in which they can learn and show mastery of the material in the class. Teachers may want to ask students for ideas about alternative projects or products.

- Students are more likely to become engaged with material that is optimally challenging. Classroom activities should be appropriate to their current knowledge and skill levels. Material that is either too hard or too easy is antimotivational. Ideally, teachers should deliver instruction that is just above the skill range of the students. The activity should be something the students can master, but not without effort and appropriate strategy use (Morrone & Schutz, 2000). Ideally, students should be challenged, but not frustrated, by classroom activities.

- Preassessing students can also help increase the intrinsic value of a class. Pretests allow teachers to find out what students already know about the material they are to cover in class and to ensure that students have the prerequisite skills and knowledge to be successful in the upcoming unit. An ideal pretest includes questions that all students should have mastered, as well as questions that, if answered correctly, indicate mastery of upcoming instructional objectives. Teachers can then use students' pretest results to provide instruction that is optimally matched to their level of mastery. If students have already mastered an instructional objective, allow them time to pursue interest-based enrichment opportunities, rather than giving them "more of the same."

- Most students tend to prefer activities that allow active participation or response. Activities that allow students to interact with the teacher and one another or allow them to manipulate materials are usually more intrinsically motivating. Research shows that students prefer active over passive forms of learning.

- Students also tend to enjoy activities that allow for immediate feedback. This is one reason that computer games are so popular. Immediate feedback enhances the psychological impact of the activity. When possible, teachers should strive to build opportunities for immediate feedback into classroom activities.

Increasing Overall Task Value

The following are some minor modifications that will increase the overall task value of activities for students:

- Educators should explain the purpose for lessons and assignments. At the beginning of every unit, explain why mastering these skills or learning this information is important to students. This helps students recognize how the knowledge or skills they are developing in class will (1) help them meet their own current needs or wants, (2) provide them with social rewards or opportunities for social advancement, or (3) prepare them for occupational or other future successes (Brophy, 1998).

- Teachers and parents can help students set short- and long-term academic goals. Small, short-term goals work better for younger students. It is essential that the goals are meaningful to students. It is important to talk with the students about possible goals because goals that adults value may have little meaning to children.

One key to motivating students to value a task is to capitalize on one of the three areas just discussed. *Why Try?* was developed to help parents and educators assess how a student values academic work (see Appendix A). A student can fill out this form individually or as part of a student-teacher confer-ence. The first 11 questions provide important information about what the student values and does not value about a par-ticular class. In addition, educators can modify the form to assess the perceived value that a student places on school in general by changing the word *class* to *school*. Examination of a student's responses to the first 11 questions can help teachers and counselors determine whether or not the student finds the class useful, interesting, or both, as well as why the student does or does not put forth effort to be successful in the class. This information can help a teacher to individualize an instructional approach with a particular student in order to increase motiva-tion. For example, a teacher can capitalize on a student's inter-ests to engage him or her in a particular unit. In addition, the teacher can emphasize the utility of the content for the student based on responses to the *Why Try?* worksheet.

Furthermore, the *Why Try?* worksheet represents an opportunity for students to reflect upon their values and goals. The worksheet encourages students to think seriously about how their performance in present classes can affect their future goals, as well as to articulate explicitly their reasons for choos-ing or failing to put forth effort in a class.

The final six questions go beyond the classroom or school, and ask students to reflect upon their own values, dreams, and goals. Teachers and counselors can use the responses to these questions to obtain a more complete picture of each student. In addition, these responses provide insights into a student's gen-eral values and goals, which may aid in the formation of more specific school-related goals. The *Why Try?* worksheet can be used as an assessment tool for teachers and counselors, a self-reflection tool for students, or a conversation starter for an individual conference or counseling session.

Self-Efficacy: "Am I Smart Enough?"

While valuing a task can be motivating, it may not be sufficient to turn that motivation into action. Students might believe that mathematics is important, but not believe they are capable in mathematics. They may also believe that a particular field of mathematics is too difficult for someone like themselves. Students must believe they have the skills to perform a task before they will attempt it. Students will not tackle challenging material if they do not believe they have the necessary skills to master it. Bandura (1977) coined the term *self-efficacy* to describe individuals' judgment of their capacity to perform specific activities.

Students develop this confidence in many ways, and those who are confident about their skills are more likely to engage in a variety of learning experiences. The perceptions students have about their skills influence the types of activities they select, how much they challenge themselves, and the persistence they exhibit once they are involved in the activities (Bandura, 1986). This is true for experiences ranging from participation in drama and athletic programs, to school achievement.

Past Performance: Success Breeds Success

Students' beliefs about how well they can perform are first and foremost influenced by how well they have performed in the past. Significant adults in children's lives can increase students' confidence by helping them recognize past accomplishments. In this way, success breeds success. Helping students acknowledge past growth is an important contributor toward their future growth. While this may sound simplistic, people of all ages often fail to recognize their successes and subsequently fail to realize their progress.

Motivation Tips

- Teachers and parents should consider videotaping students as they engage in various activities. By periodically reviewing the recordings, students can recognize how much they have improved. For example, a young student who has been taking piano lessons for several years may not feel like he has made any progress. However, if his parents have videotaped him practicing over the years and show him the tape, the student will likely be amazed at how much better he now plays. This technique can be used with any activity where visible progress can be documented.

- Educators and parents should keep samples of previous academic work and periodically review students' earlier work with them to show growth and improvement. Students are amazed at how easy their earlier work now appears and how much better they are now able to perform. Student portfolios are a popular educational practice that promotes this activity. Students can be encouraged to select work to include in their portfolios for future review.

- Educators and parents can encourage students to compete with themselves. This can be accomplished by charting progress. This might include a running list of words they know how to spell or multiplication facts they have mastered. Most children remember their parents reserving a special spot in their home to mark their height each year, and they love to observe how much taller they are becoming. Just as with the height chart, parents and teachers can also help children recognize other forms of growth and development.

Feedback: Attributing Success

The way in which parents and teachers compliment students has an impact on how successful students perceive themselves. Everyone agrees that students should be encouraged to work hard, as effort plays a significant role in achievement. However, students also need to believe they have the skills to succeed. The key is to help gifted students recognize that skills are developed and that they have acquired the skills necessary to succeed. The feedback must contain (1) recognition of the talent and (2) attribution of its development to the student.

Dweck (1999) demonstrated that students who believe abilities can be developed and are not fixed are more likely to attempt challenging tasks and persevere through difficulties than students who believe abilities are innate. Students who hold a performance orientation approach new situations as opportunities to show what they know, and they tend to believe that abilities are fixed. Therefore, they view any mistake as evidence that they lack ability. One the other hand, students who have a learning orientation view new situations as opportunities to acquire new skills or improve their existing skills.

They tend to believe that abilities are malleable, which makes them more likely to tackle difficult tasks.

Although Dweck (1999) found that elementary students already gravitate toward one or the other of these orientations, she also found that these orientations are susceptible to change. There is some evidence that changing students' attitudes about their abilities increases student achievement as much as teaching them study skills (Gordon, 2004).

Gifted students are at risk of developing a performance orientation, which may limit their willingness to take academic risks. This may be particularly true when their giftedness has not been discussed with them. Consider being identified as gifted and placed in a gifted and talented program. Now, imagine that no one discusses what this new label means or how you became gifted. As educators and parents, we are often uncomfortable discussing with children how they became gifted. This may stem from the fact that we may be wrestling with the debate over the role genetics and environment play in giftedness. Although giftedness certainly goes beyond an IQ score, we do know that genetics and environment play equally important roles in determining IQ (Neisser et al., 1996). Environment plays a slightly greater role during the early years, and genetics becomes slightly more related as we grow older (Neisser et al.; Petrill, 2003).

Students may believe they had very little to do with their giftedness. It is something that people believe about them, but they are not sure how they "got" it. If students also hold a performance orientation, they may be reluctant to participate in challenging activities for two reasons. First, they may suffer from imposter syndrome. Students may be thinking, "Everyone doesn't know how dumb I really am, and as long as I don't fail, they won't." For these students, not trying is preserving an image. They do not perceive "not trying" as poor performance. They can always say, "It wasn't important" or "I just rushed through it and didn't do my best." A second category of students are those who believe their giftedness was something they magically inherited. If they attempt a difficult task and fail, it means they aren't gifted. This logic occurs because they fail to recognize they developed their gifts and talents.

While it is true that gifted students often acquire skills more quickly and easily than their peers, they still gain such skills through learning. They may have taught themselves to read or learned to read easily at an early age, but they still learned to read. They were not born reading. It is important for gifted students to recognize that the talents they possess are acquired and that they are capable of further developing these talents.

Gifted students also need to understand that just because they find something difficult does not mean they are not smart. Young people often believe that, if they need to work hard at school, then they are not smart. In fact, peers often perceive hard-working students as less intelligent than students who do well in school without making any visible effort. Attributing success to ability or effort is a fine line to walk. The key is to acknowledge the ability while recognizing that effort went into its development. Educators and parents can help students recognize the important role both ability and effort play in talent development. One way to achieve this is through the comments made to children.

Parents and teachers should compliment students on the specific skills they have developed by drawing attention to the skill and its development. This can easily be accomplished by recognizing the skill as something the student developed. This acknowledges the effort without drawing undue attention to it. An example is "You did very well on this math project. You've learned how to solve equations."

A general compliment such as "Good work" doesn't carry the weight of something more specific such as "You have really developed the ability to provide supporting sentences for the topic sentence in your paragraphs." Students are better able to cognitively appraise their progress when feedback is specific.

The latter lets students know two things: the specific skill they possess and that they developed it. Both components are necessary. Students will reflect on the comment and think, "Yes, I have learned to write a well-organized paragraph."

Earlier research (Siegle, 1995) found that students' mathematics confidence could be increased in as little as 4 weeks by drawing attention to their progress and asking teachers to provide specific comments. However, changes in their achievement were not seen over that short period. Current research provides preliminary evidence that modifying specific comments to include a component that the student developed the skill results in increases in motivation and performance. While the specificity draws attention to what the student knows, the developmental aspect serves two purposes. First, it helps the student recognize that skills are acquired. Second, it gives the student credit for learning the skills. In other words, it helps students recognize their role in the learning process.

Of course, compliments must be genuine and earned. Complimenting children for tasks they did not perform well or for unchallenging tasks can be counterproductive and diminish their trust. When teachers and parents compliment students for sloppy or unchallenging work, students may ask themselves, "Does he really think that this is the best I can do?" Overly effusive and too numerous compliments can backfire. The goal should be to help students recognize their developed skills, not to heap undue praise.

Motivation Tips

- Educators and parents should provide specific, rather than general, comments about student work whenever possible.

- Comments should also include recognition of the development of the talent. Females often attribute their successes to hard work, rather than ability. While effort is important for success, young people must also believe they have the skills to succeed. For example, gifted girls need to recognize they can be good at math. They need to hear from caring adults that they are good at specific math skills. They, like all children, need to believe they succeed because they have the skills and put forth effort.

- Educators and parents can help students attribute their poor performance to lack of effort. While success ought to be attributed to a combination of ability and effort, poor performance should be solely attributed to limited effort. This helps student recognize the important role effort plays. It also helps them realize that effort builds ability.

Vicarious Experiences: Observing

Students also develop confidence through observing others. The most powerful models are other students, although self-modeling is also effective. Simply observing a peer accomplish a task isn't enough. For peers to be effective models, young people must believe they are similar to them (Bandura, 1982). Observing an outstanding student succeed does very little to increase the confidence of other students who perceive they have lesser ability. "Sure, she can do it. It's easy for her. She's smart." However, observing someone who is perceived as equally or less skilled succeed can have a powerful positive effect. "Wow. If he can do it, anyone can do it!" If young people believe they have similar skills, then seeing their peers succeed will increase their own confidence. If they don't feel as qualified, they are likely to say, "I'm not as good at that."

Observing peers fail can also have an impact. If students observe someone who they feel has similar or superior skills fail, they probably will have limited confidence when attempting the same task. If they observe someone with inferior skills fail, the failure will have a limited impact. Following this line of reasoning, gifted students are not necessarily effective achievement models for other students. This is particularly true for students who have not been identified as gifted and talented and who hold a performance orientation. However, almost all students in a class are neutral or effective models for increasing gifted students' confidence.

Motivation Tips

- Students need to equate effort with reward. Adults should share how their successes are built on effort. Models who verbalize their coping strategies can be more effective than models who appear to glide through a task easily (Meichenbaum, 1971). Making tasks appear effortless does nothing to increase motivation and can actually be intimidating. Children learn valuable lessons when they observe perseverance followed by success. Effective role models do not appear perfect. They show that effort pays off with reward.

- Bibliotherapy is a popular counseling strategy. Students gain confidence and motivation when they read about famous people who overcame hardships. Dweck (1999) was able to move elementary students from a performance orientation to a learning orientation by exposing them to biographies that described how eminent individuals developed their skills and talents. She also produced a reverse pattern when she exposed elementary students to biographies that focused on the natural talents of eminent individuals.

- Teachers and parents should expose students to achieving individuals with whom they can relate. Rimm (1995) found that role models are an important component in student motivation. As noted earlier, students must see themselves as similar to the role model and they must view the role model as having some power or prestige. While parents and teachers are ideal, scout leaders, coaches, and others are other possible role models.

Environmental Perception: "Can I Be Successful Here?"

As was previously discussed, students need to value the task and be confident that they have the skills to pursue it. While these two factors are powerful influences on motivation, a third component is necessary: Students must also view their environment as friendly and likely to provide positive outcomes for them. If students are to do well, at the minimum they must believe that environmental factors such as school personnel or the curriculum do not prevent them from being successful. Students who possess positive environmental perceptions believe their home and school environments support their efforts. Their perception of the friendliness of their surroundings has an impact on their academic attitude and behavior.

Ogbu (1978) noted that students expend effort where they perceive their chances of success are better. Students who grow up in a community where music is prevalent will see people around them developing their musical skills and being successful. They are more likely to pursue a musical career than someone without that experience. Unfortunately, many young people grow up in impoverished environments where resources for talent development are limited. Many times, those who do become successful leave for more lucrative opportunities, and the valuable role they could be playing as community role models is vacant.

Mickelson (1990) reported that "academic achievement is linked to students' accurate assessments of the returns that their education is likely to bring them as they make the transition to adulthood" (p. 45). It is not enough to be confident that they have certain skills; they must expect that they will succeed if they put forth effort. Phrases such as "You don't understand" or "I can't learn this way" are strong indicators that students do not view their learning environment as friendly. In other words, they don't believe they can succeed even if they try. Rathvon (1996) hypothesized that "the underachiever's failure to assume responsibility arises from his unconscious belief that his own efforts do not affect the events or individuals in his world" (p. 66).

Gifted underachievers often view school negatively (McCoach & Siegle, 2001). They may feel like they do not fit into the system, and, in some cases, giftedness can actually represent a stigma in school (Cross, 1997). Gifted students, like other students, wish to avoid embarrassment and "look good" in front of their peers. They often report that classroom teachers don't call on them when their hands are raised or embarrass them by calling on them when no one else knows the answer. From a teacher's perspective, the gifted child may appear the most likely choice to call on when no one else raises a hand. However, if the gifted child is unable to answer correctly, he or she may feel embarrassed; on the other hand, if he or she constantly answers the most difficult questions correctly, teasing by others may ensue.

A second area of concern is how teachers relate to gifted students in their classes. Rather than appreciating the special gifts and talents these students exhibit, some teachers are threatened by the presence of gifted students in their classroom.

Therefore, in some situations, low motivation may represent a coping strategy whereby students strive to adapt to an anti-intellectual school environment (Cross, 1997). Classroom activities or the curriculum may also not be appropriate for gifted students. They may be bored because they have already mastered much of the material that is being covered (Plucker & McIntire, 1996).

For the past three decades, educators have been concerned with providing gifted students with academic challenge, which has come to mean more advanced information. This might include more complex tasks within a topic area, or it might include different assignments at a higher level. Our experience has been that not all gifted students wish to be academically challenged. This is particularly true when the challenge does not originate with the student. Just because the classroom teacher wants Jon to do more challenging mathematics does not guarantee that Jon is interested in doing more challenging mathematics. Academically challenging material is not necessarily motivating to students.

Rather than striving solely for academically challenging material, educators should seek to provide students with intellectually stimulating material, as the two are not necessarily synonymous. Academic challenge is a component of intellectual stimulation, but intellectual stimulation involves more than challenging material. Content that is intellectually stimulating is novel and personally meaningful. It has a level of complexity. It often involves ambiguity, uncertainty, and unanswered questions. There is a passion and urgency about it. It may involve a situational interest that is generated by certain conditions or concrete objects in the environment, or a personal interest that drives an individual to pursue knowledge and skills. Intellectually stimulating content promotes discussion, usually involves big ideas, does not have a content ceiling, involves higher level cognition, includes multiple perspectives, does not have a single path to a solution, and the definition of the problem may vary. This material must lie within the student's zone of proximal development, and it often is taught inductively (McCoach & Siegle, 1999).

Many gifted students in school are starved for intellectual stimulation. Educators need to strive for a balance between academic challenge and intellectual stimulation.

- Too little academic challenge and too little intellectual stimulation produce bored students.

- Too much academic challenge and too little intellectual stimulation produce "turned-off" students.

- Too much academic challenge with adequate intellectual stimulation produces frustrated students.

- Optimal challenge combined with intellectual stimulation produces students in a state of "flow"(Csikszentmihalyi, 1990, 1997; Shernoff, Csikszentmihalyi, Schneider, & Shernoff, 2003).

Motivation Tips

- To the extent that teachers treat their students as if they already are enthusiastic learners, students will be more likely to become such learners (Brophy, 1998). When introducing a new concept or activity, educators can tell students how that activity will be enjoyable or interesting. For example, when introducing a more complex topic, they can refer to it as more interesting and intriguing, rather than as more difficult.

- Educators should modify instruction and the curriculum for optimal challenge. Classroom activities should be appropriate to students' current knowledge and skill levels. Material that is either too hard or too easy is antimotivational. Ideally, teachers should deliver instruction that is "just above the skill range of the students. This helps to ensure that the task is something that the students can master, but not without effort and appropriate strategy use" (Morrone & Schutz, 2000). Educators should ensure that their students are challenged, but not frustrated, by classroom activities.

- Educators should examine their instructional format. Many teachers' instructional styles do not promote the higher level thinking that gifted students need. Educators should examine how they can teach the curriculum in an intellectually stimulating fashion. They should consider the characteristics of intellectual stimulation discussed earlier.

Perceptions of the Environment and Necessary Changes

Students' perception of the friendliness of the environment may or may not be accurate. But, if they are, then changes need to be made.

Research on change has indicated that the person being asked to change must be involved in the process (Emerick, 1992). Therefore, the student should be consulted about how to rectify the environment. For example, if a child feels it is too noisy to study at home, adults can ask what needs to be done to make it quieter. It may be as simple as asking, "What would it take for you to do well?" It is important that students be involved in helping find solutions to the environmental roadblocks they perceive for two reasons. First, it enhances a sense of internal control. Second, it documents for them that something will be changing.

When consulting students about how their environment might be modified, active and empathetic listening on the part of the parent or teacher is crucial. Active listening is a powerful tool. Chances are that those who influence us most are powerful listeners. Whether instinctively or through practice, good listeners have developed the skill of empathy.

Pickering (1986) identified four characteristics of empathetic listeners: (1) desire to be other-directed, rather than to project one's own feelings and ideas onto the other; (2) desire to be nondefensive, rather than to protect the self (when the self is being protected, it is difficult to focus on another person); (3) desire to imagine the roles, perspectives, or experiences of the other, rather than assuming they are the same as one's own; and (4) desire to listen as a receiver, not as a critic, and desire to understand the other person, rather than to achieve either agreement from or change in that person.

The steps of active listening are: (1) providing verbal or nonverbal awareness of the other (i.e., eye contact); (2) responding to a person's basic verbal message; (3) reflecting feelings, experiences, or content that has been heard or perceived through cues; (4) offering a tentative interpretation about the other's feelings, desires, or meanings; (5) bringing together in some way feelings and experiences—providing a focus; (6) questioning in a supportive way that requests more information or attempts to clear up confusions; (7) sharing perceptions of the other's ideas or feelings and disclosing relevant personal information; (8) showing warmth and caring in one's own individual way; (9) finding out if interpretations and perceptions are valid and accurate; and (10) giving the other time to think, as well as to talk (Pickering, 1986).

When faced with an unfriendly environment, Sternberg (2001) outlined three possible responses: (1) modifying one's behavior to be successful in that environment, (2) changing the environment, or (3) abandoning the situation. Gifted children who underachieve in school may fail to select options that maximize their likelihood for success. There are times when the curriculum is inappropriate for a gifted student, and this may require the teacher to modify the curriculum to better match the student's academic level or learning style. Perhaps a student has already mastered her multiplication tables. In this situation, endless practice worksheets of multiplication facts are senseless. An environmental change is required in this situation. If a gifted student has not mastered his multiplication facts, the student needs to modify his behavior and put some effort into learning them since multiplication facts are basic arithmetic skills that are useful throughout life. Perhaps a student has a learning difficulty that is limiting her ability to master multiplication facts. If modifying the environment by teaching the facts in different ways doesn't work and if extensive effort on the student's part is ineffective, it may be better to abandon the task and move on. For the time being, the student could consult a completed multiplication grid when solving mathematics problems. There are also cases where a student and teacher "fail to connect" from day one. The wise solution may be to abandon the situation and move the student to another class. The key to success is assessing when to change, when to expect others to change, and when to move on.

Environmental perceptions go beyond the classroom. Cultural and economic factors may also be limiting student opportunities. Students' perceptions about the fairness of "the system" or of society in general impact their motivation. Steele (2000) reported that students may have difficulty trusting the environment and their achievement may be less influenced by their perceived abilities than their perception of the fairness of the environment. Steele randomly assigned a group of students to one of two groups. He told one group that individuals with their characteristic did not do as well on a given task as individuals without this characteristic. He said nothing to the other group that also possessed the characteristic. He asked both groups to perform a task. Those who were told they possessed the referential characteristic performed much worse on the task than those for whom nothing was stated. Steele labeled the phenomenon "stereotype threat." His work has been replicated using race, gender, age, and even athletic characteristics with both academic and physical tasks.

Motivation Tips

- Educators and parents can discuss with students the obstacles they believe are keeping them from doing well and what options exist for them. This includes a discussion of what is within the students' control, as well as what is beyond their control. Teaching students to appreciate multiple viewpoints should be part of the discussion. Educators and parents can share Sternberg's (2001) options for change with students. They can help students understand when it is important "to stand their ground," when compromise might better serve their interests, or when ignoring the situation is the best course of action.

- Educators and parents should avoid letting students use their environment as an excuse. At times, young people may attribute their failures to their environment, rather than to themselves. When this occurs, a technique such as active listening (Pickering, 1986) can unravel students' concerns.

Self-Regulation: "How Do I Put It All Together?"

The factors of task value, self-efficacy, and environmental perceptions are critical for motivation. But, being motivated may not be sufficient to remain engaged in and complete the task. A student may feel that math is important, believe that he or she can do well in mathematics, and like the school and teachers, but not follow through and execute the math assignment. It is in this regard that self-regulation is crucial.

Self-regulation strategies can be classified into three categories: (1) self-management strategies, (2) personal standards, and (3) self-monitoring.

Self-Management Strategies

Many gifted students may lack self-management strategies such as time-management and study skills. Because gifted students often progress through the early years of school without being challenged, they sometimes fail to develop the self-management skills that other students master. In the early grades, good memory and fast processing skills can compensate for note taking and other study skills. Often, educators attempt to teach students study skills before students need those skills to be successful. This process usually frustrates both the teachers and the students. Self-regulatory skills are more likely to be internalized when they are needed to solve the problem at hand. A solution to the problem is to provide gifted students with an academically challenging curriculum early and throughout their school careers so they have opportunities to develop self-management skills.

Motivation Tips

- If students are not being academically challenged, teachers should encourage them to explore opportunities to interact with more challenging and interesting material. Curriculum compacting (Reis, Burns, & Renzulli, 1992; Starko, 1986), an effective process to use with gifted students, provides a way to give students credit for their knowledge and skills and buys time to pursue more challenging content. Teachers can pretest students and determine which content they have already mastered. While other students are working on this material, the compacted student can work on more appropriate content.

- Teachers should evaluate what study skills are needed to be successful. A word of caution: Teaching study skills to gifted and talented students when they don't need them is counterproductive. Some common study skills include note taking, outlining, and using memory mnemonics. A list of note-taking strategies is included in Appendix B.

- Teachers and parents can help students organize their work and study time (see Appendix C). Greene (2001) recommended that students create a homework book to record upcoming assignments, projects, tests, and events. They should use a designated two-pocket travel folder in which one side is labeled "To Do" and the other is labeled "Done." Keeping all their important notices and papers in one place saves them time. Students can create reminder checklists, one called "At School" and one "At Home." Organizing all handouts and papers in chronological order in subject notebooks can also be helpful. Students should pack their book bag each night before they go to bed, making sure they include all of their homework. This makes it easier to remember forgotten items and eases the morning rush. The book bag should be kept in the same place every night.

Personal Standards

Another aspect of self-regulation involves setting personal standards. Some students may feel that what they are doing is "good enough." If students haven't been academically challenged in the past, they may believe they can achieve satisfactory results with very little effort. Siegle and Reis (1998) reported much weaker relationships between gifted students' perceptions of the effort they put into a subject and their performance in that subject than they reported for their ability in a subject and their performance in the subject.

Gifted students may also underachieve to hide their need for perfection. "The underachiever's perfectionistic goals also undermine her efforts to improve because they focus on the product rather than the process of learning" (Rathvon, 1996, p. 77). Gifted students may be more vulnerable because they, more than any other group, approximate perfection to a higher degree, are more often rewarded for it through their accomplishments, and often come to believe perfection is possible. Perfectionistic students often tend to be black and white about success and achievement. They either want to complete an activity perfectly or they don't want to take part at all.

Students may also have a low-risk comfort level. Perhaps the benefits of achieving don't outweigh the risks since many students believe that having to work hard means they aren't smart. As discussed earlier, students who view ability as fixed will view challenging tasks as tests of their intelligence. Conversely, students who believe that intelligence is malleable and can be developed will view challenging tasks as opportunities for improvement (Dweck, 1975). These students' reticence to achieve may be a defense mechanism to maintain their "gifted status."

Motivation Tips

- Teachers and parents should encourage students to pursue excellence, rather than perfection. Adults can model acceptance of their mistakes while striving for excellence. Gifted students should not be expected, or expect, to complete every task in every area with 100% accuracy. Educators and parents should never say, "You're suppose to be gifted" when a student makes a mistake.

- Once again, reading biographies about the failures of famous people is beneficial. For example, Abraham Lincoln started out as a captain at the beginning of the Blackhawk War; by the end of the war, he had been demoted to private. The obstacles he overcame on the road to the Presidency are impressive: failed in business in 1831; defeated for legislature in 1832; second failure in business in 1833; suffered nervous breakdown in 1836; defeated for speaker in 1838; defeated for elector in 1840; defeated for Congress in 1848; defeated for vice president in 1856; defeated for Senate in 1858; and elected president in 1860.

Self-Monitoring

Self-monitoring skills include monitoring distractibility, practicing delayed gratification, and awareness of performance avoidance. The Premack principle (also known as "Grandma's rule") applies here. The principle says that a more preferred activity can be used as a reward for a less preferred activity. Someone may enjoy exercising, but not writing. Therefore, he exercises only after he has written a preset number of pages. Parents often mistakenly reverse Premack's principle, which renders it ineffective. "Okay, I'll let you watch 30 minutes of television and then you need to start your homework" does not work as well as "As soon as you finish your homework, you may watch 30 minutes of television."

Students with a mastery orientation, which was described earlier, may demonstrate performance avoidance. Such students are motivated by generous reinforcement for success. They respond better to assignments that have detailed instructions with specific grading criteria.

Motivation Tips

- Educators and parents can help students plan schoolwork tasks. This serves two functions. First, it develops a mindset that the task is doable. Young people are often reluctant to begin a task because they are unsure how to begin. Second, it minimizes the unknown. Through planning, students can visualize a task coming to fruition. The degree of necessary task planning will vary among individuals.

- Teachers and parents can teach students to set attainable short-term goals and reward themselves once they are completed. This includes learning to withhold the reward if the task is not completed. For example, a student might reward herself with a half-hour of conversation on the phone with a friend after reading a chapter for social studies homework.

- When working with performance-avoidance students, teachers should provide detailed assignment instructions and include an evaluation rubric when appropriate. Larger tasks should be divided into smaller tasks, and the student's performance at each step should be recognized. These students may also respond positively if their desks are near the teacher's desk.

- Educators and parents can help students set realistic expectations. This involves setting goals that are difficult enough to be challenging, yet not so difficult as to be unachievable and discouraging. Learning occurs best when new material cannot be mastered without assistance, but can be mastered with minor direction from someone more knowledgeable (Vygotsky, 1939/1962).

Final Thoughts

Much of what motivates children is still a mystery. The suggestions presented in this publication provide insights into some strategies that promote motivation and an achievement orientation that will encourage students to pursue their interests and passions. With a concerted effort, educators and parents can help students to see that what they are doing serves a purpose, to believe they have the skills to perform well, to trust their environment will encourage their productivity, and to set realistic expectations for themselves. Early encouragement of these behaviors is a major step toward helping young people lead productive and fulfilling lives.

Bruns, J. H. (1992). *They can but they don't: Helping students overcome work inhibition.* New York: Penguin.

Coil, C. (1994). *Becoming an achiever: A student guide.* Marion, IL: Pieces of Learning.

Covington, M. V., & Teel, K. M. (1996). *Overcoming student failure: Changing motives and incentives for learning.* Washington, DC: American Psychological Association.

Heacox, D. (1991). *Up from underachievement: How teachers, students, and parents can work together to promote student success.* Minneapolis, MN: Free Spirit.

McCombs, B. (1996). *Motivating hard to reach students.* Washington, DC: American Psychological Association.

Rimm, S. (1995). *Why bright kids get poor grades and what you can do about it.* New York: Crown.

Rimm, S. (2003). *See Jane win for girls: A smart girl's guide to success.* Minneapolis, MN: Free Spirit.

Weinstein, C. E., & Hume, L. M. (1998). *Study strategies for life-long learning.* Washington, DC: American Psychological Association.

Zimmerman, B. J., Bonner, S., & Kovach, R. (1996). *Developing self-regulated learners: Beyond achievement to self-efficacy.* Washington, DC: American Psychological Association.

References

Bandura, A. (1977). Self-efficacy: Toward a unifying theory of behavioral change. *Psychological Review, 84*, 191–215.

Bandura, A. (1982). Self-efficacy mechanism in human agency. *American Psychologist, 37*, 122–147.

Bandura, A. (1986). *Social foundations of thought and action: A social cognitive theory.* Englewood Cliffs, NJ: Prentice Hall.

Baum, S. M., Renzulli, J. S., & Hébert, T. P. (1995). Reversing underachievement: Creative productivity as a systematic intervention. *Gifted Child Quarterly, 39*, 224–235.

Boggiano, A. K., & Pittman, T. S. (Eds.). (1992). *Achievement and motivation: A social-developmental perspective.* New York: Cambridge University Press.

Brophy, J. (1998). *Motivating students to learn.* Boston: McGraw-Hill.

Cross, T. L. (1997). Psychological and social aspects of educating gifted students. *Peabody Journal of Education, 72*, 180–200.

Csikszentmihalyi, M. (1990). *Flow: The psychology of optimal experience.* New York: HarperCollins.

Csikszentmihalyi, M. (1997). *Finding flow: The psychology of engagement with everyday life.* New York: BasicBooks.

Deci, E. L., & Ryan, R. M. (1985). *Intrinsic motivation and self-determination in human behavior.* New York: Plenum.

Dweck, C. S. (1975). The role of expectations and attributions in the alleviation of learned helplessness. *Journal of Personality and Social Psychology, 31,* 674–685.

Dweck, C. S. (1999). *Self-theories: Their role in motivation, personality, and development.* Philadelphia, PA: Psychology Press.

Eccles, J. S., & Wigfield, A. (1995). In the mind of the actor: The structure of adolescents' achievement task values and expectancy-related beliefs. *Personality and Social Psychology Bulletin, 21,* 215–225.

Emerick. L. J. (1992). Academic underachievement among the gifted: Students' perceptions of factors that reverse the pattern. *Gifted Child Quarterly, 36,* 140–146.

Gordon, E. (2004). *The development of high levels of academic ability in minority students.* Paper presented at the National Research Center on the Gifted and Talented Javits Conference, Washington, DC.

Greene, M. (2001). *Improving academic achievement: Self-regulation intervention* [CD-ROM]. Storrs: The National Research Center on the Gifted and Talented, University of Connecticut.

Hidi, S., & Harackiewicz, J. M. (2000). Motivating the academically unmotivated: A critical issue for the 21st century. *Review of Educational Research, 70,* 151–179.

McCoach, D. B., & Siegle, D. (1999, November). *Academic challenge: Are we barking up the wrong tree?* Paper presented at the annual meeting of the National Association for Gifted Children, Albuquerque, NM.

McCoach, D. B., & Siegle, D. (2001, April). *Factors that differentiate gifted achievers from gifted underachievers.* Paper presented at the annual conference of the American Educational Research Association, Seattle.

Meichenbaum, D. H. (1971). Examination of model characteristics in reducing avoidance behavior. *Journal of Personality and Social Psychology, 17,* 298–307.

Mickelson, R. A. (1990). The attitude-achievement paradox among Black adolescents. *Sociology of Education, 63,* 44–61.

Moon, S. M., & Hall, A. S. (1998). Family therapy with intellectually and creatively gifted children. *Journal of Marital and Family Therapy, 24,* 59–80.

Morrone, A. S., & Schutz, P. A. (2000). Promoting achievement motivation. In K. M. Minke & G. Bear (Eds.), *Preventing school problems—Promoting school success: Strategies and programs that work* (pp. 143–169). Bethesda, MD: NASP Publications.

Neisser, U., Boodoo, G., Bouchard, T. J., Jr., Boykin, A. W., Brady, N., Ceci, S. J., et al. (1996). Intelligence: Knowns and unknowns. *American Psychologist, 51*(2), 77–101.

Ogbu, J. U. (1978). *Minority education and caste.* New York: Academic Press.

Peterson, J. S. (2000). A follow-up study of one group of achievers and underachievers four years after high school graduation. *Roeper Review, 22,* 217–224.

Petrill, S. A. (2003). The development of intelligence: Behavioral genetic approaches. In R. J. Sternberg, J. Lautrey, & T. I. Lubart (Eds.), *Models of intelligence: International perspectives* (pp. 81–89). Washington, DC: American Psychological Association.

Pickering, M. (1986). Communication. *EXPLORATIONS, A Journal of Research of the University of Maine, 3*(1), 16–19.

Pintrich, P. R., & Schunk, D. H. (1996). *Motivation in education: Theory, research, and applications.* Englewood Cliffs, NJ: Merrill.

Plucker, J. A., & McIntire, J. (1996). Academic survivability in high-potential, middle school students. *Gifted Child Quarterly, 40,* 7–14.

Rathvon, N. (1996). *The unmotivated child: Helping your under-achiever become a successful student.* New York: Simon and Schuster.

Reis, S. M., Burns, D. E., & Renzulli, J. S. (1992). *Curriculum compacting: The complete guide to modifying the regular curriculum for high ability students.* Mansfield Center, CT: Creative Learning Press.

Rimm, S. (1995). *Why bright kids get poor grades and what you can do about it.* New York: Crown.

Rimm, S. (2001, December). Parents as role models and mentors. *Parenting for High Potential,* 14–15, 27.

Shernoff, D. J., Csikszentmihalyi, M., Schneider, B., & Shernoff, E.S. (2003). Student engagement in high school classrooms from the perspective of flow theory. *School Psychology Quarterly, 18,* 158–176.

Siegle, D. (1995). *Effects of teacher training in student self-efficacy on student mathematics self-efficacy and student mathematics achievement.* Unpublished doctoral dissertation, University of Connecticut, Storrs.

Siegle, D., & McCoach, D. B. (2002). Promoting a positive achievement attitude with gifted and talented students. In M. Neihart, S. M. Reis, N. M. Robinson, & S. Moon (Eds.), *The social and emotional development of gifted children: What do we know?* (pp. 237–249). Waco, TX: Prufrock Press.

Siegle, D., & Reis, S. M. (1998). Gender differences in teacher and student perceptions of gifted students' ability. *Gifted Child Quarterly, 42,* 39–48.

Starko, A. J. (1986). *It's about time: Inservice strategies for curriculum compacting.* Mansfield Center, CT: Creative Learning Press.

Steele, C. (2000, September). *Promoting educational success: Social and cultural considerations.* Paper presented at the U.S. Department of Education and The National Academies' Millennium Conference, Washington, DC.

Sternberg, R. J. (2001). *Successful intelligence.* Boise, ID: Annual Edufest Institute.

Vygotsky, L. S. (1962). *Thought and language.* Cambridge: Massachusetts Institute of Technology. (Original work published 1939)

Wigfield, A. (1994). The role of children's achievement values in the self-regulation of their learning outcomes. In D. H. Schunk & B. J. Zimmerman (Eds.), *Self-regulation of learning and performance: Issues and educational applications* (pp. 101–124). Mahwah, NJ: Erlbaum.

Appendix A: Why Try?

Why TRY?

Directions:
Please complete all of the following sentences regarding a class where you wish to improve your grade. There are no right or wrong answers. Put down the first idea that comes into your head. When you are finished, give this form back to your teacher.

1. When I try hard in this class, it's because

    _____.

2. I would spend more time on my schoolwork if

    _____.

3. If I do poorly in this class, then

    _____.

4. When I don't try hard in this class, it's because

    _____.

5. I would rather do _____
    than do my work for this class.

6. Doing well in this class will help me to

    _____.

7. Doing poorly in this class will keep me from

    _____.

8. This class is important because

   _____.

9. The most interesting thing that I learned this year is

   _____.

10. The thing that I am most interested in learning more
    about is _____.

11. The most interesting thing that I learned in class is

    _____.

12. I feel best about myself when

    _____.

13. I feel worst about myself when

    _____.

14. I am most proud of

    _____.

15. I wish that I could

    _____.

16. When I grow up, I want to

    _____.

17. I really value

    _____.

Created by D. Betsy McCoach for The National Research Center on the Gifted Improving Academic Achievement Study.

Appendix B: Active Study Checklist

RECITE

___ I describe or explain the topic out loud in my own words.

___ I record into a tape-recorder.

___ I teach or explain the information to someone else.

___ I role-play a part.

___ I simulate the lesson.

___ I recite the answers to questions on the topic that I made up myself.

WRITE

___ I make a chapter study review by writing key points on index cards.

___ I make and use flashcards for short-answer questions or concepts.

___ I make lists of related information by categories.

___ I draw a diagram, map, sketch, timeline, or chart from memory, and then I check the book for accuracy.

___ I write questions I think will be on the test and recite the answers.

___ I create semantic maps (visual representation of ideas) to summarize the unit (webs, sequence chains, Venn diagrams).

___ I use mnemonics to remember information.

___ I rewrite class notes, rearranging the information in my own words.

VISUALIZE

___ I close my eyes and picture in my mind what I am trying to remember (chart, map, event, scene, experiment, character).

___ I try to remember where information is located on a page.

___ I picture in my mind how the test will look based on previous similar tests.

___ I organize and design graphic organizers to put abstract information into concrete and visual form.

___ I represent concepts with symbols so I can remember them.

Created by Meredith Greene for The National Research Center on the Gifted Improving Academic Achievement Study.

Appendix C: Note-Taking Tips

The very act of writing something down may improve your retention of that information. Note taking also increases concentration. Here are some tips for better note taking:

____ Write titles and headings on the page correctly.

____ Label all notes in a notebook with date, topic, and page.

____ Leave a wide margin so you can add questions, comments, or new information to it later; make a wide left margin as the recall column.

____ Skip lines between subtopics.

____ Circle, underline, or highlight key phrases in the notebook when studying.

____ Interact with the notes soon after taking them; review them, transcribe them into a different form, recite them.

To take notes from a textbook:

____ Use the chapter format to guide you (headings, text boxes, chapter summaries, questions).

____ Skim the whole section before beginning your note taking.

____ Write in your own words what you read.

____ Describe a sequence of events, steps, or ideas.

___ List main topics and subtopics in outline form.

___ List details for each main idea and subtopic.

___ Make semantic map (graphic organizer) for main ideas and subtopics.

___ Categorize details.

___ Write a summary for each section.

To take notes from a classroom discussion:

___ Use the tips above.

___ Write in your own words what is said. Don't try to write down every word.

___ Invent a personal form of shorthand of symbols and abbreviations for common words or phrases.

___ Use arrows, stars, or asterisks to indicate most important points.

___ Practice good listening techniques: Look directly at the speaker, do not talk when the speaker is talking, think along with the speaker.

___ Listen for key phrases such as "There are 3 reasons," "In conclusion," and "An important point is . . ."

Created by Meredith Greene for The National Research Center on the Gifted Improving Academic Achievement Study.

Del Siegle is an associate professor in gifted and talented education in the Neag School of Education at the University of Connecticut, where he coordinates the Three Summers master's degree and online graduate classes. He teaches courses in educational research, creativity, and technology. He serves on the executive board of the National Association for Gifted Children and the board of directors of The Association for the Gifted. In 2001, Dr. Siegle was named Early Leader by the National Association for Gifted Children. Prior to earning his Ph.D. in gifted education, he developed and taught in a gifted and talented program in Montana. Dr. Siegle conducts workshops nationally and internationally on topics related to gifted education. His research interests include student motivation, teacher biases in identifying gifted students, and teaching with technology.

D. Betsy McCoach is an assistant professor in the Educational Psychology Department at the University of Connecticut, where she teaches graduate courses in measurement, statistics, and gifted education. Dr. McCoach completed her Ph.D. in educational psychology with concentrations in gifted education, school psychology, and quantitative research methodology at the University of Connecticut. Previously, she was a teacher of the gifted and a secondary gifted specialist in Pennsylvania. She was a recipient of a Spencer Doctoral Fellowship from the American Educational Research Association for the 2001–2002 academic year. In addition, she received an AERA Dissertation Research Grant for the 2002–2003 academic year. Dr. McCoach's areas of research interest include the underachievement of gifted students, gifted students with dual exceptionalities, motivation, instrument design and analysis, modeling students' academic growth, and quantitative research methodology.

Printed in the United States
by Baker & Taylor Publisher Services